Armored Vehicles

Kate Riggs

CREATIVE EDUCATION • CREATIVE PAPERBACKS

Published by Creative Education and Creative Paperbacks
P.O. Box 227, Mankato, Minnesota 56002
Creative Education and Creative Paperbacks
are imprints of The Creative Company
www.thecreativecompany.us

Design by Ellen Huber; production by Blue Design
Art direction by Rita Marshall
Printed in the United States of America

Photographs by Corbis (Shane A. Cuomo/US Army/Reuters),
Dreamstime (Goce Ristesk), Flickr (The U.S. Army), Getty
Images (VANDERLEI ALMEIDA), iStockphoto (breckeni,
ewg3D, JaiGieEse), Shutterstock (Creativa Images,
OlegDoroshin, yuri4u80)

Library of Congress Cataloging-in-Publication Data
Riggs, Kate.
Armored vehicles / Kate Riggs.
p. cm. — (Seedlings)
Includes index.
Summary: A kindergarten-level introduction to armored
vehicles, covering their crew, weapons, role in battle, and such
defining features as their wheels.
ISBN 978-1-60818-659-4 (hardcover)
ISBN 978-1-62832-244-6 (pbk)
ISBN 978-1-56660-673-8 (eBook)
1. Armored vehicles, Military—Juvenile literature. I. Title.

UG446.5.R544 2015
623.74'75—dc23   2015007402

CCSS: RI.K.1, 2, 3, 4, 5, 6, 7; RI.1.1,
2, 3, 4, 5, 6, 7; RF.K.1, 3; RF.1.1

First Edition HC 9 8 7 6 5 4 3 2 1
First Edition PBK 9 8 7 6 5 4 3 2 1

TABLE OF CONTENTS

Time to move!

Armored vehicles carry troops onto battlefields. They go where tanks (above) go.

Fighting vehicles do not have as much armor as tanks.

But they can hold
more people.

Soldiers inside the vehicle can fire **weapons**.

A main gun is on top of the vehicle.

One person drives the vehicle.

Another keeps a lookout for anything dangerous.

Some fighting vehicles have eight wheels. Others have more wheels and tracks.

An armored vehicle carries fighters to a new place.

It drives over rough ground. It tries to keep people safe.

Go, armored vehicle, go!

Picture an Armored Vehicle

light

hatch

hull

gun

track

wheel

armored: describing a metal covering that keeps something safe

tracks: big, strong belts that go around a vehicle's wheels

weapons: things like guns or bombs used to guard or hurt others

Read More

Alvarez, Carlos. *Strykers*.
Minneapolis: Bellwether Media, 2011.

David, Jack. *M2A2 Bradleys*.
Minneapolis: Bellwether Media, 2009.

Websites

Army Coloring Pages
http://www.hellokids.com/r_709/coloring-pages
/transportation-coloring-pages/army-vehicles-coloring-pages
Print out a picture of an armored vehicle to color, or color
it online.

U.S. Army Vehicles
http://www.goarmy.com/army-videos.sch
-Army%20Vehicles.html
Watch videos about the Stryker and other fighting vehicles.

Index